Great Women in History

Helen Keller

by Erin Edison

Consulting Editor: Gail Saunders-Smith, PhD

CAPSTONE PRESS
a capstone imprint

Pebble Books are published by Capstone Press,
1710 Roe Crest Drive, North Mankato, Minnesota 56003.
www.capstonepub.com

Library of Congress Cataloging-in-Publication Data
Cataloging-in-Publication information is on file with the Library of Congress.
ISBN 978-1-4765-4217-1 (library binding)
ISBN 978-1-4765-5165-4 (paperback)
ISBN 978-1-4765-6022-9 (ebook PDF)

Editorial Credits
Erika L. Shores, editor; Gene Bentdahl, designer; Marcie Spence, media researcher;
Laura Manthe, production specialist

Photo Credits
Alamy Images: Everett Collection, 8, INTERFOTO, 6, 10; AP Images: 12, RK, 4;
Corbis: Bettmann, 18; Getty Images: Hulton Archive, 20, Imagno, 16, Topical Press
Agency, 14; Newscom: CSU Archives/Everett Collection, cover, Everett Collection, 1;
Shutterstock: maximum, design element

Note to Parents and Teachers

The Great Women in History set supports national social studies
standards related to people and culture. This book describes
and illustrates Helen Keller. The images support early readers in
understanding the text. The repetition of words and phrases helps
early readers learn new words. This book also introduces early
readers to subject-specific vocabulary words, which are defined
in the Glossary section. Early readers may need assistance to read
some words and to use the Table of Contents, Glossary, Read More,
Internet Sites, and Index sections of the book.

Printed in the United States of America in North Mankato, Minnesota.
092013   007764CGS14

Table of Contents

1880

born

Early Life

Helen Keller was an author and an activist for the blind. Helen was born in Alabama in 1880. She became very sick when she was 19 months old. The illness left her blind and deaf. She could not see, hear, or talk.

Helen in 1946

1880

born

Young Helen often misbehaved.
She bit or pinched. She was angry.
Helen couldn't talk to other people
or understand them. Her parents didn't
punish her though. They knew
Helen didn't understand the world
around her.

 Helen in 1887

1880

born

1887

meets Anne
Sullivan

Helen's parents wanted her to learn to communicate. The Kellers hired Anne Sullivan to teach 6-year-old Helen. Anne had been nearly blind as a child. She learned how to read braille. She also knew sign language.

◀ Helen (left) and Anne Sullivan

1880

born

1887

meets Anne
Sullivan

Education

Anne began by spelling out words into Helen's palm. Helen soon learned that everything she touched had a name. Helen then could communicate by spelling back into Anne's hand.

 Helen (left) and Anne Sullivan

1880
born

1887
meets Anne
Sullivan

1904
graduates
college

Anne taught Helen to write. Helen also learned to read braille books.

In 1896 Helen went to school.

Then in 1900 Helen went to Radcliffe College. She was the first deaf and blind person to graduate from college.

 Helen, after graduating from Radcliffe College in 1904

1880
born

1887
meets Anne Sullivan

1904
graduates college

Life's Work

Helen wanted to help people.
She worked for the American
Foundation for the Blind. She gave
speeches and wrote articles.
She asked lawmakers to think
of how laws would affect the blind.

 Helen working at her desk in 1910.

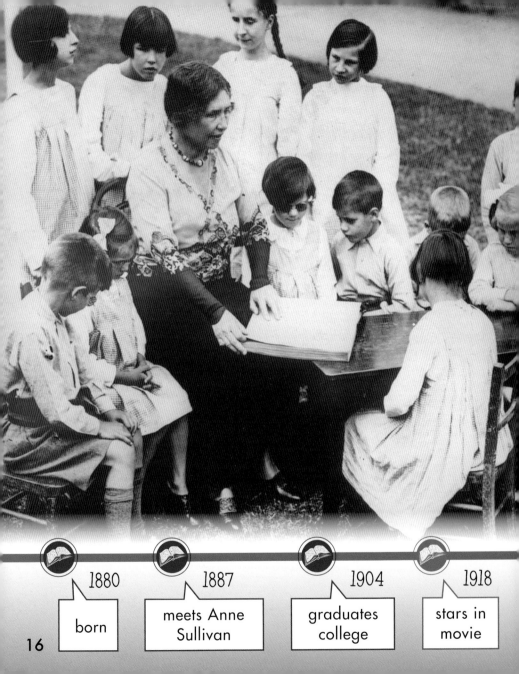

1880
born

1887
meets Anne
Sullivan

1904
graduates
college

1918
stars in
movie

16

Helen wrote 12 books during her life.
The Story of My Life was her most
popular book. She also starred
in a movie about her life
called *Deliverance*.

 Helen reading from her own book in 1930.

1880
born

1887
meets Anne
Sullivan

1904
graduates
college

1918
stars in
movie

Later Life

Helen traveled around the world nine times. She visited 35 countries. She asked people to help the blind. She gave hope to soldiers who had lost their sight or hearing during World War II (1939–1945).

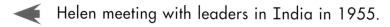

Helen meeting with leaders in India in 1955.

1943-1946

visits soldiers

1880
born

1887
meets Anne
Sullivan

1904
graduates
college

1918
stars in
movie

Helen showed the world that a deaf and blind person can do great things. President Lyndon Johnson awarded Helen the Presidential Medal of Freedom in 1964. Helen died at her home in Connecticut in 1968.

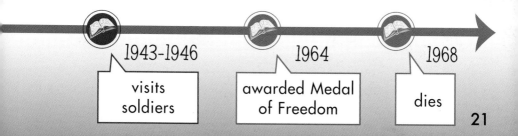

1943-1946
visits
soldiers

1964
awarded Medal
of Freedom

1968
dies

Glossary

activist—a person who works for changes in laws

braille—a set of raised dots that stand for letters and numbers; people use their fingertips to read the raised dots

college—a school that students attend after high school

communicate—the sharing of facts, ideas, or feelings with other people

foundation—an organization that gives money to good causes

graduate—to finish all the required classes at school

popular—liked or enjoyed by many people

punish—to make a person suffer for something he or she did wrong

sign language—hand signs that stand for words, letters, and numbers

soldier—a person who is in the military

Read More

Amoroso, Cynthia, and Robert B. Noyed. *Helen Keller.* Basic Biographies. Mankato, Minn.: Child's World, 2010.

Lindeen, Mary. *Leading the Way.* Wonder Readers. North Mankato, Minn.: Capstone Press, 2012.

Peck, Audrey. *Helen Keller: Miracle Child.* Beginning Biographies. New York: PowerKids Press, 2013.

Internet Sites

FactHound offers a safe, fun way to find Internet sites related to this book. All of the sites on FactHound have been researched by our staff.

Here's all you do:

Visit *www.facthound.com*

Type in this code: 9781476542171

Critical Thinking Using the Common Core

1. Why did Helen bite and pinch before she learned how to communicate? (Key Ideas and Details)

2. What made Helen a good worker for the American Foundation for the Blind? (Integration of Knowledge and Ideas)

Index

Word Count: 311
Grade: 1
Early-Intervention Level: 24